A Note to Parents and KU-593-313

DK READERS is a compelling programme for beginning readers, designed in conjunction with leading literacy experts, including Maureen Fernandes, B.Ed (Hons). Maureen has spent many years teaching literacy, both in the classroom and as a specialist in schools.

Beautiful illustrations and superb full-colour photographs combine with engaging, easy-to-read stories to offer a fresh approach to each subject in the series. Each DK READER is guaranteed to capture a child's interest while developing his or her reading skills, general knowledge and love of reading.

The five levels of DK READERS are aimed at different reading abilities, enabling you to choose the books that are exactly right for your child:

Pre-level 1: Learning to read
Level 1: Beginning to read
Level 2: Beginning to read alone
Level 3: Reading alone
Level 4: Proficient readers

The "normal" age at which a child begins to read can be anywhere from three to eight years old. Adult participation through the lower levels is very helpful for providing encouragement, discussing storylines and sounding out unfamiliar words.

No matter which level you select, you can be sure that you are helping your child learn to read, then read to learn!

LONDON, NEW YORK, MUNICH,
MELBOURNE, and DELHI

Senior Editor Helen Murray
Designer Lauren Rosier
Jacket Designer Lauren Rosier
Design Manager Ron Stobbart
Publishing Manager Catherine Saunders
Art Director Lisa Lanzarini
Publisher Simon Beecroft
Publishing Director Alex Allan
Production Editor Andy Hilliard
Production Controller Melanie Mikellides

Reading Consultant
Maureen Fernandes

This edition published for The Book People,
Hall Wood Avenue, Haydock, St. Helens WA11 9UL

This edition published in 2013
First published in Great Britain in 2013 by
Dorling Kindersley Limited
80 Strand, London WC2R 0RL
Penguin Group (UK)

Slipcase Unique ID: 001–196366–Jul/13

Page design copyright © 2013 Dorling Kindersley Limited

LEGO, the LEGO logo, the Brick and the Knob
configurations are trademarks of the LEGO Group.
© 2013 The LEGO Group
Produced by Dorling Kindersley
under license from the LEGO Group.

A CIP catalogue record for this book is available from the
British Library.

ISBN: 978-1-4093-3790-4

Colour Reproduction by Altaimage in the UK
Printed and bound in China by L. Rex Printing Co. Ltd.

Discover more at
www.dk.com
www.LEGO.com

Contents

DK READERS

PROFICIENT 4 READERS

Welcome to Heartlake City

Written by Helen Murray

Lake Heart

Heartlake City gets its name from the pretty heart-shaped lake at its centre. People go to Lake Heart to swim, fish and even ice-skate in winter.

Stephanie

Fun-loving Stephanie is always on the lookout for a new adventure. She loves to plan trips and outings for her friends.

Heartlake City

Welcome to Heartlake City! There is always something fun and exciting to do here. You could explore the boutiques and cafés on Main Street or enjoy an open-air concert in the park. Perhaps you might like to go to the pool to sunbathe and chat with friends or catch a boat to Lighthouse Island to search for buried treasure? Anything is possible in Heartlake City.

Olivia

Emma

International sporting events and talent contests are held here. If you are lucky, you might even catch a film crew shooting a movie!

The town is home to five smart, adventurous and talented best friends: Emma, Mia, Stephanie, Andrea and Olivia. They think Heartlake City is a wonderful place to live. Come and join the girls and explore their amazing home!

Emma
Fashionable Emma likes to explore the city's boutiques for cool clothes and accessories.

Stephanie

Andrea

Mia

Special offer
Hurry! There is a great deal on cupcakes at the café today!

Sunny terrace
Andrea and the girls like to sit outside on the terrace, which overlooks the beautiful Lake Heart.

A fun place to work

Whether the girls are taking a road trip along the coast, shopping on Main Street or planning an exciting event in the town, life is always fun in Heartlake City. For lucky Andrea, the fun doesn't stop when she is at her part-time job at the City Park Café. It is one of the coolest places to hang out in the city – and it is a great place to work, too!

The café is a central meeting spot for Olivia, Mia, Emma, Andrea and Stephanie.

When Andrea is not working, she meets the girls to gossip over milkshakes and cupcakes.

Andrea works as a waitress at the busy café. Her first job of the day is to put out the sign that advertises the café's amazing cupcakes.

Dish of the day
As well as cakes, the café does a great range of delicious burgers and sandwiches.

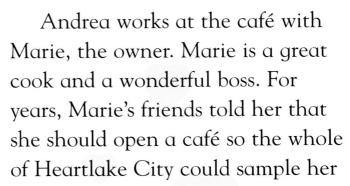

Andrea works at the café with Marie, the owner. Marie is a great cook and a wonderful boss. For years, Marie's friends told her that she should open a café so the whole of Heartlake City could sample her food – so one day she did!

Marie bakes cakes and pies before the café opens. Her favourite moment of the day is when she pulls out a tasty cake from the oven. The wonderful smell that greets her makes all the hard work worthwhile.

The café stays busy all day. Andrea and Marie rush around taking orders and delivering tasty food to eager customers.

Andrea is an amazing singer and is always dreaming about becoming a pop star, even at work! Fortunately for Andrea, Marie encourages her to perform for customers at the café.

It is quiet and peaceful, with spectacular views of the beach. It really is the ultimate place to relax!

Emma likes to spend a lazy sunny afternoon cooling off in the pool and working on her tan. Sometimes she takes a quick nap on the lounger under the shade of the umbrella. She always makes sure she has a refreshing drink or ice-cream sundae close by.

Lush setting
Emma loves the calming scent of this pretty poolside plant.

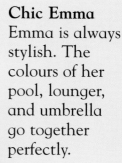

Chic Emma
Emma is always stylish. The colours of her pool, lounger, and umbrella go together perfectly.

13

Ice cream

The girls love to eat ice cream. Emma and Andrea like strawberry and vanilla best, Mia and Olivia like chocolate and Stephanie's favourite flavour is cookie dough.

Emma, Andrea, Mia, Olivia and Stephanie lead busy lives. Sometimes they need to take time out from schoolwork, hobbies and part-time jobs, so Emma invites them over to spend a day in the sun. They have fun sunbathing and paddling in the pool.

The friends sing along to cool tunes on their MP3 players and relax on the sun loungers.

Sometimes Andrea helps Emma to make delicious ice-cream sundaes for all the girls. Andrea has learned some great tips from her part-time job at the City Park Café. She likes to add her own special touch with cherries, chocolate chips and sprinkles on top. Yum!

Splash pool concert
Andrea loves to sing. She often gives her friends their own private poolside performance!

New residents
Olivia's family
recently moved
to Heartlake
City. They live
in the leafy
Heartlake
Heights area,
which overlooks
the beach and
harbour.

Home sweet home

There's so much to see and do
in Heartlake City, but sometimes
there's no place like home. And
Olivia's house is one of the coolest
in the city. The girls like to head to
Olivia's house to spend time together.

Roof terrace

Bathroom

Kitchen

Living room

16

Olivia, Andrea, Mia, Emma and Stephanie have many choices about where to go in the beautiful house. They can watch films in the comfortable living room, cook together in the spacious kitchen and stargaze at night from the roof terrace.

The friends also enjoy spending time with Olivia's parents. Anna and Peter are always there with a sympathetic ear whenever the girls have any worries.

Olivia's bedroom

Swing

Baked treats
Olivia's mum bakes cakes for the girls. Fellow baker Stephanie loves to swap recipes and tips with her.

Olivia's workshop
Olivia loves science. She has a workshop where she goes to experiment and invent.

17

Prizes

Between them, the girls have won countless trophies and prizes for their horseback riding skills. Olivia has proudly stuck her latest award on her wall.

Olivia, Emma, Mia, Stephanie and Andrea often head upstairs to Olivia's bedroom. Emma decorated the room for Olivia when she first moved in. Doesn't it look beautiful? The girls listen to music and give each other makeovers. They all crowd in front of the beautiful lighted mirror to try out new hairstyles. Sometimes they stay for sleepovers, too. Three of the girls squeeze into the bed while the other two sleep on the floor!

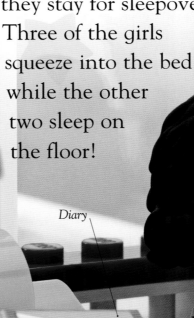

Diary

18

The girls often stay up late talking and don't always get as much sleep as they should!

Olivia loves it when her friends come to stay, but she also enjoys some quiet time once they have left. She writes about her friends, their dreams and their adventures in her diary.

Olivia's cat
Missy is very playful. Her favourite game is hide-and-seek. But it looks like Olivia has discovered Missy a little too easily this time – she is in the bathroom!

Lights

Mirror

Perfume

Dressing table

19

Olivia often invites her friends to barbecues in her front garden. Olivia's dad loves to cook outside. He grills sausages and chicken, which he coats in a delicious sauce. It is his secret recipe!

Olivia's dad always makes sure he cooks something tasty for Mia, who doesn't eat meat – she is a vegetarian. He grills delicious vegetables, which he grows in his very own vegetable patch.

Handy girl
Olivia can fix anything! She mended and repainted the letter box when her family first moved to the house.

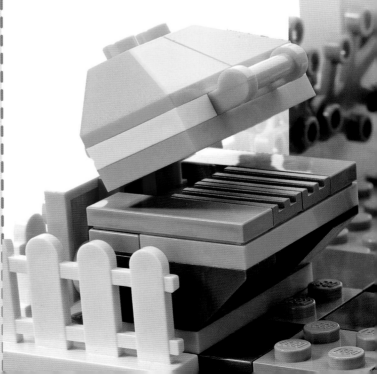

Olivia and her mum set up the table and chairs and bring plates, cutlery and ketchup from the kitchen. The barbecue is ready!

Just opposite Olivia's house is a cool treehouse where the girls go to arrange parties, make top-secret plans and camp out under the stars. They worked hard to fix and decorate the treehouse to make it a beautiful girls-only space.

The treehouse
The girls love to hang out at the treehouse in the summer. No boys and no parents are allowed!

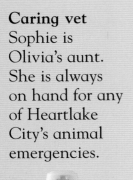

Heartlake Vet

Heartlake City is not just a great place for people to live, it is a safe and caring place for animals, too. Heartlake Vet is where all the city's sick pets and wild animals go to be nursed back to health.

All kinds of animals, from birds and hedgehogs to dogs and horses, are cared for at this friendly, modern animal hospital.

Letter box

Rescue trolley

There are different areas for the animals to recover and get well again. Large animals can rest in a recovery stall, while small animals are looked after in a cage next door.

Sophie is Heartlake City's vet. She is gentle and kind to the animals and she works very hard. Animal-loving Mia volunteers part time at the vet. She is learning how to look after the different animals.

Mia
Mia is crazy about animals. She bonds naturally with animals and is practical and very hands-on. She would make a great vet.

Large animal stall

Patient sign

Small animal cage

Tap

Medicine

Examination chart
Mia carefully records the patient's details on the chart.

The state-of-the-art surgery centre is equipped with everything. Sophie needs to work out what is wrong with the animals. Sophie gives each animal a thorough checkup on the examination table. Sometimes she takes an X-ray to check for broken bones or any other internal problems.

Feeding time
Mia feeds the animals twice a day. Some animals need to eat more than others!

Food trolley

There is a scale for monitoring the weights of each of the animals. Mia checks that the hedgehog is putting on weight. Fortunately, he is! He should be ready to be released back into the wild soon. There is also a heat lamp to warm up any poor animals that have been outside in the cold for a long time.

Aquarium
Sophie looks after Heartlake City's unwanted pet fish in this large tank. They are very pretty and colourful!

Aquarium

Phone

Reception desk

X-ray

Sink

Heat lamp

Weighing scale

25

Sophie soothes scared and timid animals with her soft voice and gentle nature.

Good hygiene
Sophie and Mia carefully clean all of the vet's tools in the sink after each use.

Sophie has all kinds of tools to monitor the animals' health and to make them feel better. She hangs a stethoscope around her neck, which she uses to listen to each animal's breathing and heartbeat. She also has a thermometer to monitor the animals' temperatures and a torch for checking their ears, too. Sophie gives the hedgehog some final checks before he can be released. She is pleased – his ears look nice and healthy!

The animal hospital is equipped with a huge variety of medicines to help each of the animals recover as quickly as possible. There are ice packs to soothe swelling and bruises and lots of bandages for broken bones and other injuries, too.

On the move
Sophie and Mia can quickly transport very sick or injured animals in the rescue trolley.

Emergency service
People call the surgery with emergencies. Sophie often rushes out of the door to visit sick pets at home.

Always prepared
Stephanie is super-organised. She always makes sure that there is plenty of food in the trailer for any rescued animals.

Daisy
This mischievous little rabbit has a habit of wandering away from her bunny house.

Stephanie helps out Sophie, the vet, by patrolling Heartlake City looking for lost or wounded pets and wild animals. She rides around on a cool quad bike, called the Pet Patrol. The bike has big, sturdy wheels, which allow her to go off-road onto bumpy terrain. Stephanie attaches a trailer to the back of the quad bike, so there is a lot of space to carry rescued animals as well as food.

When Stephanie finds injured or sick animals, she delivers them to Sophie and Mia at Heartlake Vet. But if an animal is lost, she takes it home to its owner. Sociable Stephanie makes it her business to know everyone in the city, so she doesn't usually have any difficulties locating the pets' homes!

Stephanie has found Daisy, who disappeared from her bunny house. Luckily, she knows just where Daisy lives!

Dinner time
Daisy is happy to be back in her bunny house. Stephanie gives the hungry rabbit a tasty carrot.

29

Stable chic
Emma sometimes takes her love of design to the extreme. She once decorated hay with bows to add colour to her horse's stable!

Riding camp
Stephanie, Mia and Emma often go to summer riding camp. They have lots of fun while improving their riding skills.

Heartlake horses

One of the best things about Heartlake City is that there are lots of great places to go horseback riding. Well, that's what the girls think!

Mia, Emma, Andrea, Stephanie and Olivia like to spend time at Heartlake Stables, which is located on the edge of Clover Meadows. They hone their riding and jumping skills at the stables. But for more exciting rides, they canter across the meadows and into the Whispering Woods.

Mia and Emma both have their own horses, Bella and Robin. All of the girls enjoy entering competitions, but Mia and Emma are the champion horseback riders of the group! They compete regularly in showjumping and dressage events across Heartlake City – and they usually win!

The horses at
Heartlake Stables
love to graze on
the lush grass of
Clover Meadows.

Mia's horse, Bella,
lives at Heartlake
Stables. Mia goes
there every day to feed,
groom and ride Bella.

31

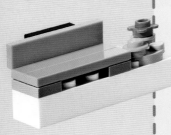

A girly day out

When Emma, Stephanie, Mia, Andrea and Olivia want to treat themselves to a day of shopping and pampering, they head to Main Street.

People-watching
Sometimes the girls need to rest their tired feet. They sit on their favourite bench and watch other shoppers pass by.

Beauty Shop

This chic shopping area is home to Heartlake City's trendiest shops, boutiques and salons.

The girls' favourite place on Main Street is Butterfly Beauty Shop. They sometimes spend a whole afternoon trying out new looks and getting pampered.

Sarah, who works at the salon, is one of the coolest people the girls know. The girls like to ask Sarah for style tips and advice. Aspiring fashion designer Emma always listens especially closely!

Sarah is an amazing make-up artist. Girls come from all over Heartlake City to have their make-up done by Sarah. She helps them to find the perfect shades for their lips, cheeks and eyes.

In the summer, Sarah offers makeovers on the street. Passers-by can't resist the hot new lipstick colours!

Make a wish
This up-market salon has a gorgeous fountain outside. The friends always make a wish as they toss a coin into the water.

Sarah
Sarah loves working at the salon. She hopes to open a salon of her very own one day.

Sarah loves to advise Emma, Stephanie, Mia, Olivia and Andrea on make-up. The girls have great fun trying out different looks before a special party or event. There is always so much choice – it is hard to know which colours to pick!

Favourite lipstick
Emma spends time trying out different lipstick colours before finally settling on her favourite.

Make-up
Butterfly Beauty Shop stocks a fantastic range of make-up. It always has the season's hottest shades.

When schoolwork, part-time jobs, and hobbies take their toll, the girls relax with a pampering session in the salon. The friends take it in turns to rest in the comfy chair while Sarah styles their hair. She keeps a close eye on the runways and fashion magazines and enjoys trying out the latest looks on the girls! Sometimes Sarah paints the girls' nails, too. The five friends always leave the salon feeling refreshed and fabulous!

Emma and Sarah chat about fashion while Sarah styles Emma's hair.

Hairdresser

The girls go to Butterfly Beauty Shop to have their hair cut and styled. Sarah is a fantastic hairdresser!

Stephanie, Olivia, Mia, Andrea and Emma like to shop for clothes and accessories, too. Butterfly Beauty Shop sells a wide range of glamorous sunglasses, hair clips and bows.

Natural talent
Emma is great at hunting down accessories to complement her friends' outfits.

Creative Emma loves to help her friends select new outfits and accessories. She always seems to know what will look just right. What will the girls buy today?

Emma is always on the lookout for design inspiration. A shopping day with her four best friends usually provides her with plenty of new ideas!

Emma's purchases
Emma loves the colour yellow at the moment. She buys a pretty yellow bow for her hair.

Olivia's bag
The purple trim on Olivia's new handbag matches her purple skirt perfectly.

Special events

One of the best things about living in Heartlake City is that there are always lots of fun and exciting events to go to. One of Mia's favourites is the annual Heartlake Dog Show. Mia loves to have the opportunity to put her animal training skills into action!

In the show's grooming area, Mia works hard preparing the puppies, Scarlett and Charlie, for the show.

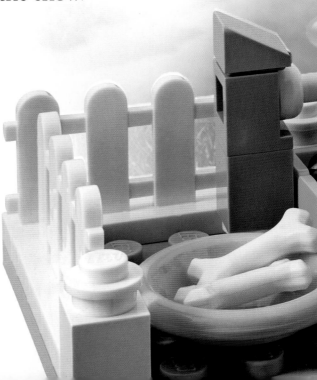

Mia scrubs the dogs with a special dog shampoo and styles their hair. The dogs don't like getting wet, but they like it when Mia gently combs their hair. For the ultimate finishing touch, Mia dresses up each puppy with a pretty purple bow.

Grooming
Mia has everything she needs to pamper Scarlett and Charlie before their big moment on the dog show stage.

39

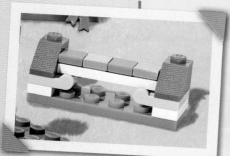

The bench
The dogs have to tread carefully as they walk along this narrow bench in the Most Agile Puppy event.

The dog show has a large obstacle course and runway where the dogs compete for prizes. There are lots of individual events in each show. This year, Charlie and Scarlett are competing for the Most Agile Puppy prize and the Cutest Puppy award. Could one of the puppies even win Best in Show?

Animal-lover Mia has a natural talent when it comes to training animals.

Grooming area

Seesaw

Charlie and Scarlett know exactly what to do in the obstacle course because Mia has taught them so well. They are sure to win a prize!

The runway
Scarlett and Charlie excitedly parade down the runway as they compete for the Cutest Puppy award.

Light

Camera

Runway

41

Official photographer
Emma takes some great shots of the happy winners.

Pretty in pink
Mia gives the puppies new pink bows to reward them for all their hard work.

Charlie and Scarlett have done it! They have won first and second place in the Most Agile Puppy event. They completed the obstacle course in the fastest times and with no mistakes. All of Mia's training has paid off! Mia can hear Olivia, Stephanie, Emma and Andrea cheering loudly in the audience. It has been a wonderful day!

The puppies stand proudly on the winners' podium while Mia excitedly gives them their awards. They have won so many ribbons that soon Mia will need to find a new place for all of the prizes!

The puppy house
Mia sticks the ribbons onto the puppy house and puts the dogs to bed. The puppies will need lots of sleep after an exciting but tiring day.

43

A born performer

Although music is her real passion, Andrea loves to dance and act, too.

The stage

Standing under the spotlights of the open-air stage, Andrea feels like a superstar!

Of all the cool things happening in Heartlake City, the girls look forward to Andrea performing on stage the most. People come from all over the city to listen to Andrea sing at an open-air concert in the park. Andrea delights the audience with her amazing talent and beautiful voice. The concert reminds Stephanie, Emma, Mia and Olivia just how lucky they are to have such a talented singer as their best friend.

Andrea has her sights set on stardom. She dreams of being spotted by a talent scout from a record label. Could today be her lucky day?

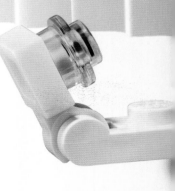

Andrea steps in front of the curtain to greet her friends and fans. She is becoming the biggest star in Heartlake City!

Songwriter
Andrea writes music at her grand piano. Performing and composing is thirsty work, so that she makes sure she always has a glass of water close by.

Outdoors-loving Olivia

Olivia is always prepared for adventure. She would never leave the house without a map or compass!

Adventure all around

The girls all share a sense of adventure. But nobody loves to plan a trip more than Stephanie, the chief organiser of the group.

The friends often hit the road in Stephanie's stylish convertible. They drive beyond the suburbs and busy Main Street area of Heartlake City to the Whispering Woods and Clearspring Mountains.

Travelling companion

Sometimes Stephanie's cute dog Coco is lucky enough to come along for the ride.

The girls hike the mountain trails to see amazing views of the city below. They also like to explore the woods, looking out for wildlife. So far, they have seen deer, rabbits, moles and beautiful butterflies. There is a rumour that bears have been seen deep inside the woods, but the friends haven't explored that far – yet!

There are still so many exciting adventures to plan in Heartlake City. Where will the five friends go next?

Musical Andrea
Andrea provides cool music for the journey – and she always sings along!

Caring Mia
Mia once brought a sick rabbit home from the woods and nursed him back to health.

Quiz

1. What is Andrea's first job of the day at the City Park Café?

2. At barbecues, why does Olivia's dad cook different meals for Mia?

3. What instrument does the vet use to listen to an animal's breathing and heartbeat?

4. What did Emma once do to decorate her horse's stable?

5. Which event did Charlie and Scarlett win at Heartlake Dog Show?

1. She puts out the sign that advertises cupcakes 2. Because Mia is a vegetarian 3. A stethoscope 4. She decorated the hay with bows 5. The Most Agile Puppy event